LIGHT

Kolawole Owomoyela

Syncterface Media
London
www.syncterfacemedia.com

Unless otherwise indicated, all Scripture quotations in this book are taken from the King James Version of the Holy Bible. Scriptures marked NKJV are taken from the New King James Version®. Copyright © 1982 by Thomas Nelson. Scriptures marked GWT are taken from God's Word Translation Copyright © 1995 by God's Word to the Nations. Used by permission of Baker Publishing Group. Scriptures marked AMP are from The Amplified Bible Copyright © 1954, 1958, 1962, 1964, 1965, 1987 by The Lockman Foundation
(Capitalised text and italics may be used for emphasis)
Used by permission.

No part of this book may be reproduced or transmitted in any form or by any means, graphic, electronic, or mechanical, including photocopying, recording, taping or by any information storage or retrieval system, without the permission of the author.

LIGHT: UNLOCKING THE MYSTERY THAT GUIDES LIFE
ISBN: 978-0-9569741-3-6
Copyright © March 2015
Kolawole Owomoyela
All Rights Reserved

Published in the United Kingdom by

Syncterface Media
London
www.syncterfacemedia.com
info@syncterfacemedia.com

Cover Design: Syncterface Media, London

This book is printed on acid-free paper

CONTENTS

Acknowledgements vii
Foreword ix
A Word From The Author xi
In The Beginning 1
God is Light 13
Expressions of Light 19
When Light Goes Dark 29
You are The Light of the World 41
Benefits of Light 49
Be Prepared 57

Acknowledgements

A heartfelt thanks to God for the grace given to complete this book. The genuine faith in my parents, Mr. & Mrs. Emmanuel Omoniyi Owomoyela, and its influence in my life is well acknowledged. Many thanks to my siblings for all their support and prayers.

A big thank you to Mrs. V.A. Oloruntegbe, who encouraged me to start publishing the teachings I have been privileged to handle. God has made this a reality at His appointed time.

I appreciate Mrs. Olajumoke Opemuti for her prayers for this project. God had from the first day placed His seal on our prayers.

To Aunty B (Mrs Bola Deola-Adewunmi), thanks for taking time to proof-read the manuscript.

To my brother Samson Dairo, I value your advice and efforts towards the completion of this book. And yes, just like you said, I am already thinking of another book if God permits.

To my Pastor, brother and friend, Pastor Tayo Adare. I am grateful for taking out time to write the foreword of this book. May God's work prosper in your hands. Amen

To my darling wife and Jewel of inestimable value, IfeoluwapoA, thank you for your prayers, dedication and support always. I love you forever.

To the team at Syncterface Media, I have no regrets working with you as my publisher. You guys are no doubt a huge blessing to me.

FOREWORD

In my part of the world, there is an adage that says, "if fire is burning a man and his child, the man takes care of himself before looking for a way to deliver his child because if he is not delivered he cannot be of benefit to the child". This does not suggest cruelty but emphasizes the order of precedence when responding to situations beyond one's control.

In the story of creation in *Genesis 1:1-3*, when the earth was without form and void, the first thing on the mind of God was light. His statement, "Let there be light", was the foundation for all creation.

Wole has penned down a lot of insightful truth in the exposition of this concept of light to encourage and enlighten our understanding. He shows us that light has personality and that there are principles that govern light. He also looks at the essence of light and how the concept of light permeates the entire landscape of God's intention for Man.

Wole is a seasoned minister of the Gospel who ministers with integrity and great insight. I recommend this book to all for exhortation, edification and comfort.

May we all advance in the Light.

Tayo Adare
Lead Pastor, Faith Rest Assembly
Ibadan, Nigeria.

A Word From The Author

The concept of light is usually something most people would gloss over. When light is mentioned, many people, most likely, will not think beyond the light that lightens the day or the electrical lamp that brightens a dark room. However, when we think about "light" more closely, we are forced to try to find answers to the myriad of questions that could pop into the mind. Can light be personified or is light just a product of the Creator? Can you describe light without describing its products? Is light just a transient state? Is light more than the creation of inventors?

I believe there is more to life than it being just about living in a physical world. Though life is considered transient, it is still a journey we all need to make. A journey that requires guidance. Agreeing that life requires guidance immediately leads us to start to consider the fact that living life without guidance is like living in the dark ages. We, therefore, need light to guide us through life. The brighter the light, the less bumpy the road of life becomes.

Given the fact that light is crucial to life, it then becomes imperative for us to consider the nature and attributes of the light that is providing the guidance. We need to know who or what light is. We need to understand the operations of light. Light is life; God is light; knowledge is light; light is direction. For a Christian, light is the tool for discerning the timing of God's programme. Life cannot be lived to the fullest without Christ and we need light to lead us to Him.

These and many more wonderful truths about light are shared in this book.

Chapter 1
IN THE BEGINNING

¹ In the beginning God created the heaven and the earth.
² And the earth was without form, and void; and darkness was upon the face of the deep. And the Spirit of God moved upon the face of the waters.
³ And God said, Let there be light: and there was light.

Genesis 1:1-3

To every journey, there is a beginning. So to begin this journey of discovering the nature and attributes of light, what better place to start than by looking at the experience generally referred to as "The Beginning"? I believe that God's programme for humanity is locked up in this experience of "The Beginning" and if we are able to unlock this treasure chest, the gems we discover will be life changing.

It is possible you have observed from the scriptures how Jesus referred to principles that were set forth in the beginning; redefining concepts the people had given other interpretations other than what was originally intended.

For example, in Matthew's gospel, we come across a story of the Pharisees tempting Jesus by asking him questions about marriage and divorce. Jesus' response showed them that Moses allowed them to divorce because of the hardness of their hearts, **but from the beginning it was not so** (*Matthew 19:8*). In other words, there was no provision for divorce according to God's original plan. Without an understanding of the original intent of marriage at the onset, an understanding of this fundamental principle that guides marriage would have been absent and many, like the Pharisees, would not have understood that a view superior to the one Moses gave in the law existed.

The deeper we look into scriptures, the more we realise that marriage is actually an institution meant to mirror the union between Christ and the Church. Jesus can never divorce, his bride, the Church. Marriage will only be enjoyed if we understand the depths of Christ's love for the Church and how the Church in turn should submit to Him. Divorce would not be an item on the menu if husbands love their wives just as Christ loves the Church and wives submit to their husbands just as the Church is subject to the authority of Christ. Today, marriages are under attack even in the body of Christ. We need to go back to the beginning to understand God's purpose for marriage.

In another place, in *Matthew 5,21–48*, we see Jesus taking topical issues of the time, and indeed, still relevant today and addressing them with the wisdom of someone living under the influence of the light we are discussing. Jesus' mission was not to destroy the Law or the Prophets, but to fulfil it. He redefined mis-understood topical issues like Murder, Adultery, Marriage, Oaths, Restitution (*the law that said "an eye for an eye" was simply meant for restitution; paying the price for the damage done and not for vengeance or retaliation as it appears in its literal sense*) and Love.

Something quite fascinating is the way Jesus articulated his response to each one of these topics. He started explaining each one by saying "*You have heard that it was said, …But I say to you..*"

²¹ Ye have heard that it was said of them of old time, Thou shalt not kill; and whosoever shall kill shall be in danger of the judgment: *²² But I say unto you*, That whosoever is angry with his brother without a cause shall be in danger of the judgment: and whosoever shall say to his brother, Raca, shall be in danger of the council: but whosoever shall say, Thou fool, shall be in danger of hell fire.

Matthew 5:21-22

²⁷ Ye have heard that it was said by them of old time, Thou shalt not commit adultery:
²⁸ But I say unto you, That whosoever looketh on a woman to lust after her hath committed adultery with her already in his heart.

Matthew 5:27-28

³¹ It hath been said, Whosoever shall put away his wife, let him give her a writing of divorcement:
³² But I say unto you, That whosoever shall put away his wife, saving for the cause of fornication, causeth her to commit adultery: and whosoever shall marry her that is divorced committeth adultery.

Matthew 5:31-32

³⁸ Ye have heard that it hath been said, An eye for an eye, and a tooth for a tooth:
³⁹ But I say unto you, That ye resist not evil: but whosoever shall smite thee on thy right cheek, turn to him the other also.

Matthew 5:38-39

⁴³ Ye have heard that it hath been said, Thou shalt love thy neighbour, and hate thine enemy.
⁴⁴ But I say unto you, Love your enemies, bless them that curse you, do good to them that hate you, and pray for them which despitefully use you, and persecute you;

Matthew 5:43-44

The Beginning is a Person

The beginning goes beyond just being the point at which something starts. It is not just the state of things. I believe it is represented in the person of Christ. Some may find it hard to get their minds around this concept but the Beginning is Christ.

Let us look at some of these scriptures.

> [8] *I am Alpha and Omega, the beginning and the ending, saith the Lord, which is, and which was, and which is to come, the Almighty.*
>
> Revelation 1:8

> [6] *And he said unto me, It is done. I am Alpha and Omega, the beginning and the end. I will give unto him that is athirst of the fountain of the water of life freely.*
>
> Revelation 21:6

> [13] *I am Alpha and Omega, the beginning and the end, the first and the last.*
>
> Revelation 22:13

The totality of God's plan is represented in Christ. He is all that God is saying and doing. Nothing exists outside of Him. He is before all, in all and after all.

> [1] **In the beginning was the Word**, *and the Word was with God,* **and the Word was God.**
> [2] *The same was in the beginning with God.*
> [3] *All things were made by him; and* **without him was not any thing made that was made.**
>
> John 1:1-3

The beginning is therefore not an event. God is the beginning. John the Beloved, in his epistle, referred to the beginning, and his writing revealed that Genesis 1 is not just giving an account of creation, but also testifying about the Creator. Let us look at the story again.

> [1] *"In the beginning God created the heaven and the earth.*
> [2] *And the earth was without form, and void; and darkness was upon the face of the deep. And the Spirit of God moved upon the face of the waters".*
>
> Genesis 1:1-2

Then God introduced light.

³ *"And God said, Let there be light: and there was light".*

Genesis 1:3

Darkness prevailed before the creation of the heavens and the earth. Heaven was without light, and the earth was waste and empty. What a joy to know that Light illuminates. This Light [*the true, genuine, perfect and steadfast light*] was introduced in the beginning so that the ultimate programme of God will be revealed. God caused light to shine in darkness and the intent of His heart became a reality.

All Beginnings start with light

Everything has a beginning for us humans. For most people, the words "let there be light" are usually attributed to situations where there is a power outage or when someone turns off the lights in a room but when you look at the story in Genesis a bit more closely, you realise that the first light God created was not the light used for separating day and night. That came on the fourth day.

> ¹⁴ *And God said, Let there be lights in the firmament of the heaven to divide the day from the night; and let them be for signs, and for seasons, and for days, and years:*
> ¹⁵ *And let them be for lights in the firmament of the heaven to give light upon the earth: and it was so.*
> ¹⁶ *And God made two great lights; the greater light to rule the day, and the lesser light to rule the night: he made the stars also.*
> ¹⁷ *And God set them in the firmament of the heaven to give light upon the earth,*
> ¹⁸ *And to rule over the day and over the night, and to divide the light from the darkness: and God saw that it was good.*
> ¹⁹ *And the evening and the morning were the fourth day.*
>
> *Genesis 1:14-19*

This is very intriguing. So if "let there be light" did not refer to the light that gives us day and night, what then did it refer to? Well, let us see what God said immediately after making the statement.

> *⁴ And God saw the light, that it was good: and God divided the light from the darkness*
> *⁵ And God called the light Day, and the darkness he called Night.* **And the evening and the morning were the first day.**
>
> Genesis 1:4-5

I believe this day and night is what Jesus, thousands of years later, spoke of when He said, in *John 9:4*, *"I must work the works of him that sent me,* **while it is day: the night cometh, when no man can work**.*"* So "day" is linked to the time when people can work. Without light being divided from darkness like God did, it is difficult to work because it is this light that removes ignorance, confusion, sin or misery. It makes your path shine brighter and brighter until the perfect day. Just as light revealed the state of the earth before creation, the new life experience does not really start until, this light, Christ is recognised as the starting authority in the life of an individual or an organisation. Let us look at the stories of Jeremiah the prophet and Paul the Apostle.

The Prophet Jeremiah had a vision of the condition of Judaea during the Babylonian captivity. It was similar to the beginning before creation.

> *"I beheld the earth, and, lo, it was without form, and void; and the heavens, and they had no light".*
>
> Jeremiah 4:23

There was disorder in the entire nation of Israel. There was no light. The years of captivity were years of darkness and it continued until the appointed time when the LORD stirred up the spirit of Cyrus king of Persia. In other words, God enlightened his mind and showed him what he was meant to do and a burning desire to see to the performance of God's bidding.

> *¹ Now in the first year of Cyrus king of Persia, that the word of the Lord by the mouth of Jeremiah might be fulfilled, the Lord stirred up the spirit of Cyrus king of Persia, that he made a proclamation throughout all his kingdom, and put it also in writing, saying,*
>
> Ezra 1:1

Light was needed to lead Israel out of captivity. When light comes, it will make you free. *"And you shall know the truth and the truth shall make you free"* – John 8:32

The story of the salvation of Saul of Tarsus is a little more dramatic than the story of the prophet Jeremiah mentioned above. God could have arranged Saul's encounter differently but He chose to make him encounter light. As he journeyed to Damascus to persecute the followers of the Way, **a light from heaven shone around him and he fell to the ground**. Following this encounter, the light of God flooded his entire being and brought him to a point of realisation of his spiritual blindness and ignorance. He got access to and unlocked the mysteries that others before him did not know. He received grace to make people see what the fellowship of the mystery was, which was hidden in God **from the beginning.**

> *¹For this cause I Paul, the prisoner of Jesus Christ for you Gentiles,*
> *² If ye have heard of the dispensation of the grace of God which is given me to you-ward:*
> *³ How that by revelation he made known unto me the mystery; (as I wrote afore in few words,*
> *⁴ Whereby, when ye read, ye may understand my knowledge in the mystery of Christ)*
> *⁵ Which in other ages was not made known unto the sons of men, as it is now revealed unto his holy apostles and prophets by the Spirit;*
> *⁶ That the Gentiles should be fellowheirs, and of the same body, and*

> partakers of his promise in Christ by the gospel:
> ⁷ Whereof I was made a minister, according to the gift of the grace of God given unto me by the effectual working of his power.
> ⁸ Unto me, who am less than the least of all saints, is this grace given, that I should preach among the Gentiles the unsearchable riches of Christ;
> ⁹ And to make all men see what is the fellowship of the mystery, which from the beginning of the world hath been hid in God, who created all things by Jesus Christ:
> ¹⁰ To the intent that now unto the principalities and powers in heavenly places might be known by the church the manifold wisdom of God,
> ¹¹ According to the eternal purpose which he purposed in Christ Jesus our Lord:
> ¹² In whom we have boldness and access with confidence by the faith of him.
>
> Ephesians 3:1-12

The impact of this light on Saul, later called Paul, was so great as is evidenced in the deep truths of the Gospel he brought to light. He understood the will of God and lived to fulfil it. He fought the good fight of faith and he finished the race that was set before him.

One of the key challenges for us today is to consider whether or not we have had an encounter with the light of God. At the point we come to the saving knowledge of God through Christ Jesus, the light of God floods our hearts. Paul described this experience by saying, we become partakers of the inheritance of the saints in the light:

> ¹² giving thanks to the Father who has qualified us to be partakers of the inheritance of the saints in the light.
> ¹³ He has delivered us from the power of darkness and conveyed us into the kingdom of the Son of His love,

> Colossians 1:12-13

> *"For you were once darkness, but now you are light in the Lord. Walk as children of light".*
>
> Ephesians 5:8

The Apostle Paul was not the only apostle that referred to the association we should have with light. Peter the Apostle also said;

> *"But you are a chosen generation, a royal priesthood, a holy nation, His own special people, that you may proclaim the praises of Him who has called you out of darkness into His marvellous light"*
>
> 1 Peter 2:9

God has called us into His marvellous light. His light is wonderful. It is not the usual light we see around. We also, like Paul, can have access to the mystery of God's Kingdom when His light shines upon us. Concerning these mysteries that are freely given to us, Paul wrote saying, *"Eyes have not seen, nor ear heard, neither have entered into the heart of man, the things which God has prepared for them that love Him.* **But God has revealed them unto us by His Spirit**: *for the Spirit searches the deep things, yes, the deep things of God"* – 1 Corinthians 2:9-10.

What is called a mystery has been revealed by God Himself who concealed it! Paul did not describe the mysteries as myths we cannot access; rather they are accessible truths revealed by God through His Spirit who searches the deep things and reveals them to us. The deep is usually vast, dark and obscure, difficult to penetrate but what a privilege we have in His light.

For the person who embraces the light, the change it brings to their life is as different as light is from darkness. The presence of Christ in our lives is synonymous with the presence of this great and wonderful Light.

Jesus' mission was to be a great Light

Immediately Jesus started His ministry at Capernaum in the regions of Zebulun and Naphtali, He fulfilled the prophecy of Isaiah in *Isaiah 9:1-2*

> [15] "Land of Zebulun and land of Naphtali, the Way of the Sea, beyond the Jordan, Galilee of the Gentiles—
> [16] **the people living in darkness have seen a great light;** on those living in the land of the shadow of death a light has dawned."
>
> Matthew 4:15-16 (NIV)

Jesus' presence in the cities meant illumination. One of the important aspects of this mission was the ability to ensure that the light was transferable such that after his departure, His followers would also be in a position to bring joy to many cities and situations. The presence of His followers was supposed to have an effect similar to that of someone opening a bottle of perfume in a room and having the fragrance of the perfume fill the room.

However, before you can get yourself into a position where you can let the light shine through you, like it did with the followers of Jesus, you need to be like a luminous object that absorbs light when exposed to it and emits the light when in darkness.

> [12] *Restore to me the joy of Your salvation, And uphold me by Your generous Spirit.*
> [13] *Then I will teach transgressors Your ways, And sinners shall be converted to You.*
>
> Psalm 51:12-13 (NKJV)

Our mission also needs to be similar to what Jesus did. He became a light to many. Do we represent light to the darkness around us? Are we helping those in darkness see light or are we letting the god of the world, the devil, keep them in darkness?

You can start your encounter with light now

We were all brought forth in iniquity and conceived in sin (*Psalm 51:5*). We were all born spiritually blind and the works of Jesus (*John 9:4*) is the salvation of our souls and the healing of our spiritual blindness. Are you reading this book and you are yet to experience the saving knowledge of God? You need to accept Christ now so that you will be translated from darkness to light.

After Jesus healed the man who was born blind as recorded in *John 9*, He asked him, *"Do you believe in the Son of God?" (John 9:35)*. All you need to do is to believe in the Son of God. I dare to ask you the same question today. *"Do you believe in the Son of God?"*

If your answer to the question is no, go ahead and confess with your mouth the Lord Jesus and believe in your heart that God has raised Him from the dead, then you will be saved and the light of God will flood your being because you will be translated from darkness to light. As you continue in Him, your paths will be like a shining light that shines more and more unto a perfect day (*Proverbs 4:18*).

Chapter 2
GOD IS LIGHT

"This then is the message which we have heard of him, and declare unto you, that God is light, and in him is no darkness at all".

1 John 1:5

God's message for mankind is simply the message of light. As we saw in the previous chapter, Jesus' mission included being a light to those who are in darkness. A core part of the message of God to humanity is this message of light because He desires that man is well guided in life. No one can walk through darkness unless they are guided. The same way a blind person needs a guide, they that live in darkness need light and for everyone that is already in the light, there is room for the brighter light.

The message we have heard from Him is that God is light. God is the object of communication. The uniqueness of the message is summed up in the assertion that God is light. Indeed, God is light and in Him is no darkness at all! No, not even a speck of darkness; gloominess; obscurity; ignorance; error; untruthfulness; misery; sin; or death can be found in Him. There is no variation or shadow of turning in Him.

> [17] *Every good gift and every perfect gift is from above, and cometh down from the Father of lights, with whom is no variableness, neither shadow of turning.*
>
> *James 1:17*

Light is the insignia of truth, knowledge and purity. All

of which signifies the personality of God. The absence of darkness in God depicts Him as the ultimate light. This message of God being light is not something new that I have coined. It is also a message that has existed from the beginning. God through Jesus described himself as light.

> [1] **That which was from the beginning**, which we have heard, which we have seen with our eyes, which we have looked upon, and our hands have handled, concerning the Word of life—
> [2] the life was manifested, and we have seen, and bear witness, and declare to you that eternal life which was with the Father and was manifested to us—
> [3] that which we have seen and heard we declare to you, that you also may have fellowship with us; and truly our fellowship is with the Father and with His Son Jesus Christ.
> [4] And these things we write to you that your joy may be full.
> [5] This is the message which we have heard from Him and declare to you, that God is light and in Him is no darkness at all.
>
> 1 John 1: 1-5 (NKJV)
>
> [12] Jesus spoke to the Pharisees again. He said, "I am the light of the world. Whoever follows me will have a life filled with light and will never live in the dark."
>
> John 8:12 (GW)

What do you think the world will be like without Christ? I think it will be like the original state of the earth before creation – formless, dark and empty. The world will be full of evil, hatred, misery and confusion everywhere at a level that cannot be compared to anything we are seeing now. In fact, everything indeed will be meaningless just like the Preacher said in *Ecclesiastes 1:2* which says, "Vanity of vanities, saith the Preacher, vanity of vanities; all is vanity."

Someone may ask, what exactly do you mean when you

say "He is light"? A good way of answering questions like this is to tell stories. Let us look at the story that gives the context in which Jesus declared Himself as the light of the world. A woman has been caught in the very act of adultery. An act which was clearly against the laws of God. In fact, the law says the penalty for such an act is death.

> [10] *And the man that committeth adultery with another man's wife, even he that committeth adultery with his neighbour's wife,* **the adulterer and the adulteress shall surely be put to death.**
>
> *Leviticus 20:10*

Imagine how she must have grown pale as she stood face-to-face with, the ultimate penalty, death. Night came upon her, as she surely would have uttered her last prayers. Darkness loomed but something marvellous happened.

> [10] *When Jesus had lifted up himself, and saw none but the woman, he said unto her, Woman, where are those thine accusers? hath no man condemned thee?*
> [11] *She said, No man, Lord. And Jesus said unto her, Neither do I condemn thee: go, and sin no more.*
>
> *John 8:10-11*

The dark clouds faded away and gave way for light. Hope was restored as Jesus gave her another opportunity to live. Her face brightened and she left rejoicing but in the midst of the joy, Jesus warned her not to sin anymore. Men sought for the condemnation of the adulteress but Jesus validated the scripture which says '*For God did not send His Son into the world to condemn the world, but that the world through Him might be saved*' (John 3:17). Paul, in his letter to the Romans said, "*there is no condemnation for as many who are in Christ Jesus...*' (Romans 8: 1-2). Condemnation is when we refuse to acknowledge light.

Jesus, in *John 3:19* said, *'this is the condemnation that has come into the world, that men loved darkness rather than light, because their deeds were evil'* –

Do you see what light does? Light is not condemning, rather it is revealing. Imagine what would have happened to this woman if the light of the world was missing. This gives you an idea of the kind of solutions we should be bringing to the world. How bright the world would be if we let our let shine.

Jesus came to the world to lighten up mankind. He came to give hope to humanity. He came to give life to us, even life in abundance (*John 10:10*). His mission was to

> [18] *The Spirit of the Lord is upon me, because he hath anointed me to preach the gospel to the poor; he hath sent me to heal the brokenhearted, to preach deliverance to the captives, and recovering of sight to the blind, to set at liberty them that are bruised,*
> [19] *To preach the acceptable year of the Lord.*
>
> Luke 4:18-19

God's Covenant with Light

Even though we have said, that God is Light, we can also see another perspective of light being a product of God with which He has chosen to make a covenant. God has made an everlasting covenant with light – **it will endure forever.** Scriptures reveal that words associated with light are not quantifiable when measured with time.

For instance, the Psalmist says that light (***sun and moon***) shall endure throughout all generations:

> [5] *They shall fear You As long as the sun and moon endure, Throughout all generations*
>
> Psalm 72:5 (NKJV)

> [36] *His seed shall endure forever, And his throne as the sun before Me;*
>
> Psalm 89:36

God's covenant with light is sure, so is God's covenant with you. Israel and Judah were away in captivity and God made a covenant with them which He communicated through Jeremiah His prophet. Israel would not only return to their land but true worship will also be restored. This covenant did not sound realistic to them. They had gone astray; Jerusalem was besieged by Nebudchadnezzar, one of the major monarchies of the time, their houses and fields were burnt and left desolate.

Despite these dire times they found themselves in, God still wanted His chosen people, Israel, to understand that a covenant existed and this covenant was a sure guarantee that they would be delivered. How amazing that God used his covenant with light to describe the covenant He had with Israel.

> [35] *Thus says the LORD, who gives the sun for a light by day, the ordinances of the moon and the stars for a light by night, who disturbs the sea, and its waves roar (The LORD of hosts is His name):*
> [36] *"If those ordinances depart from before Me, says the LORD, then the seed of Israel shall also cease from being a nation before Me forever."*
>
> Jeremiah 31:35-36

> [25] *Thus saith the Lord;* ***If my covenant be not with day and night, and if I have not appointed the ordinances of heaven and earth;***
> [26] *Then will I cast away the seed of Jacob and David my servant, so that I will not take any of his seed to be rulers over the seed of Abraham, Isaac, and Jacob: for I will cause their captivity to return, and have mercy on them.*
>
> Jeremiah 33:25-26

Of all things God created, it was light He used to explain

that His covenant is irrevocable. Have you heard God's promise and still wondered how God would do what He said He would do? I agree, sometimes when we hear God's promises to us, they sound so wonderful and almost unbelievable but we have to remember that God's ways and our ways are not the same.

Mary the mother of Jesus felt the same way too. She was a virgin, yet an angel of the Lord said she would conceive and give birth to a son without having intercourse with a man. Just thinking of this again makes me imagine how unbelievable this would have sounded back then without all the advancements we have today. Even today, believing a promise of this magnitude is not quite as easy as you might think. Our mind will quickly process the words and ask– *how can this be*? Mary asked the same question too. That is what makes Him the Almighty God. God is able to do what He has said. His covenants are irreversible. His promises are yea and Amen. His words are faithful and true.

Chapter 3
EXPRESSIONS OF LIGHT

Today through technology, man has been able to convert light into different forms of energy in order to sustain life. Light is essential, not only for humans but also for plants. Plants need light, humans also need the light of the sun for essential minerals that aid healthy living. Without light death will be inevitable. This shows that the very life we live is dependent on light. High death rate during winter is a well-reported trend throughout the colder regions of the earth. Energy bills increase drastically during these times because life must be sustained.

Light is life

Light does not just exist out of nothing. The existence of light signifies life. You only need to look out of the window of an aeroplane as it makes its descent as it approaches the airport and behold the many lights that start to become obvious to remember that all those lights must be maintained by a form of life.

Every human should be a beacon of light. A lighthouse that gives people in darkness the confidence that all is well. A lighthouse that gives hope to the desperate. The more you think about this concept of a lighthouse, you wonder who is responsible for managing the strong beams of light that come from the lighthouse. In like manner, you may wonder the source of the light that shines in you. The good news is that we do not need to go far. The bible explains the source of the light. Look at these two scriptures.

> "In him was life; and the life was the light of men".
>
> John 1:4

> [14] "Therefore He says, Awake you who sleep, arise from the dead, and Christ will give you light."
>
> Ephesians 5:14

Even to a dead man, the scriptures say that Christ will give light. The prophecy of Isaiah *(Isaiah 9:1-2)* reported in *Matthew 3:15-16* also confirmed this – *"...And upon those who sat in the region and shadow of death Light has dawned."* Nothing can impact on a dead man as life. When we faint in things that pertain to God or in our relationship with Him, what we need is light, for light is life. When we are in a state of utter spiritual torpor, the voice of God through the Gospel will raise us back to life and Christ will shine on us. His life is the spiritual energy that will sustain and keep us in Him. In *Acts 17*, Paul proclaimed God to the men of Athens who raised an altar to an unknown God as the One who gives life and breath to all and that in Him - *as a result of the spiritual energy we derive from Him* - we live, and move and have our being.

> [23] *For as I passed by, and beheld your devotions, I found an altar with this inscription, TO THE UNKNOWN GOD. Whom therefore ye ignorantly worship, him declare I unto you.*
> [24] *God that made the world and all things therein, seeing that he is Lord of heaven and earth, dwelleth not in temples made with hands;*
> [25] *Neither is worshipped with men's hands, as though he needed any thing, seeing* **he giveth to all life, and breath, and all things**;
> [26] *And hath made of one blood all nations of men for to dwell on all the face of the earth, and hath determined the times before*

appointed, and the bounds of their habitation;
²⁷ That they should seek the Lord, if haply they might feel after him, and find him, though he be not far from every one of us:
*²⁸ **For in him we live, and move, and have our being**; as certain also of your own poets have said, For we are also his offspring.*

Acts 17:23-28

Light is direction

³ O send out thy light and thy truth: let them lead me; let them bring me unto thy holy hill, and to thy tabernacles.

Psalm 43:3

When a blind man leads another blind man, they will both end up in a ditch. Driving at night is not fun for some people because they cannot see properly, but today, car manufacturers now use Xenon or high-intensity-discharge (HID) lights. They shine two or three times brighter than the normal car head lamps. Some of them have self-levelling technology while others have automatic levelling technology so that it won't blind drivers of oncoming vehicles.

In fact, some very old model car owners have changed their head lamps to Xenon lights. Reflective highway signs are more visible under this light. Light is needed for guidance and direction. Jesus said that '*if anyone walks in the day, he does not stumble because he sees the light of the world*' *(John 11:9)*. When God brought the children of Israel out of Egypt, He led them to the Promised Land with Light – a pillar of cloud by day and a pillar of fire by night. None of them knew the route He took them through. They all had to depend on and follow the light.

When we need direction from God, all we should ask for is light – "*For You will light my lamp; the LORD my God will enlighten my darkness.*" - Psalm 18:28.

Light is our guide to Christ. The news of the birth of Christ was announced to the wise men and they were led to where Jesus was laid by a shining star in the sky.

> ⁹ When they had heard the king, they departed; and, lo, the star, which they saw in the east, went before them, till it came and stood over where the young child was.
>
> *Matthew 2:9*

The Bible also records the story of an Ethiopian eunuch, who, on his way back home, after worshipping in Jerusalem, was reading the prophecy of Isaiah (*recorded in Isaiah 53:7-8*), but just did not understand it. God guided him to the truth by sending Philip to him who expounded the scriptures to him. He believed in Christ and was baptised (*Acts 8:26-39*). Similarly, the Holy Spirit will convict sinners and lead them to believing in Christ, and He will guide (direct, show, steer and lead) believers into all truth and will show us things to come (*Isaiah 11:2; John 16:13*).

Some months ago, a former high school classmate was moved by God's Spirit to ask me about knowing Jesus. Apparently, he was one of my contacts on Blackberry Messenger and my profile message at that time was culled from a hymn I love to sing - "*Knowing You, Jesus... there's no greater thing*". He had previously asked me about my relationship with God following my posts on Facebook. Reading my profile message, he humbly asked me to tell him the benefits of knowing Jesus. I spoke to him about Jesus and the Holy Spirit convinced him and that same day he said to me that he was ready to surrender his life to Christ. The light of the Gospel shone in his heart and led him to Christ. Hallelujah!

God's eternal purposes are also connected with light

> [1] The Pharisees also with the Sadducees came, and tempting desired him that he would shew them a sign from heaven.
> [2] He answered and said unto them, When it is evening, ye say, It will be fair weather: for the sky is red.
> [3] And in the morning, It will be foul weather to day: for the sky is red and lowering. O ye hypocrites, ye can discern the face of the sky; but can ye not discern the signs of the times?
>
> Matthew 16:1-3

Jesus rebuked the Pharisees and the Sadducees for their inability to discern the signs of times. The signs of times show that it is the time of the Messiah. They were blind to the events that showed the fulfilment of prophecy – the end of the Jewish dispensation and the establishment of the Kingdom of Christ.

Similarly, Jesus has told us the signs of the end of age. We need the light of God to fully discern this time as we live in it.

The Law is Light

Most of the instructions recorded in the book of proverbs came from father to son, or mother to son in some cases. The book covers the realities of human existence which will serve as a good guide for any child or adult. In one of the instructions passed to the son by the father, he likened commandment to a lamp and law as light.

> [20] My son, keep thy father's commandment, and forsake not the law of thy mother:
> [21] Bind them continually upon thine heart, and tie them about thy neck.
> [22] When thou goest, it shall lead thee; when thou sleepest, it shall keep thee; and when thou awakest, it shall talk with thee.

> ²³ For the commandment is a lamp; and the law is light; and reproofs of instruction are the way of life:
>
> Proverbs 6:20-23

The Psalmist said that God's word is a lamp to our feet and a light to our path (*Psalm 119:105*). God is the Father of light and as sons of light we are meant to pay attention to the wisdom of the Father, receive His words, and treasure His commands within us. God instructed fathers to diligently teach their children the laws. They should discuss it always and make sure that it is written all over the house. We have God's law with us which we must read and meditate on day and night. According to the above verse, the law which is light will lead us when we walk about in life with no fixed direction, it will keep us when sleep, that is, we are dormant or unconscious of some realities of life, and it will speak to us when we are awake (*completely conscious*).

Light is needed for all seasons, whether we are on the move or not. God's light is needed for every decision we make in life. Yes, every decision. David never lost a battle because he obeyed instructions. He depended on God for strategy for every battle. God's light can equally guide you in your career, business, investment, marriage, ministry, etc. As we subscribe to His light, we will discover new things and will find direction for our feet. It will be impossible to walk in error or confusion in as much as we obey God. The path of the just only shines brighter to a perfect day.

Light, a Product of Knowledge?

Knowledge is the awareness or possession of information, facts, ideas, truths or principles. The general awareness or the possession of God's truth illuminates the spirit of man. Knowledge radiates like light. Knowledge singled out Daniel in the land of captivity as he shone like a star in that dark and perverse region. He had answers to riddles and doubts. He was a problem-solver. He glowed in great brilliance because He knew God.

> [1] *Belshazzar the king made a great feast to a thousand of his lords, and drank wine before the thousand.*
> [2] *Belshazzar, whiles he tasted the wine, commanded to bring the golden and silver vessels which his father Nebuchadnezzar had taken out of the temple which was in Jerusalem; that the king, and his princes, his wives, and his concubines, might drink therein.*
> [3] *Then they brought the golden vessels that were taken out of the temple of the house of God which was at Jerusalem; and the king, and his princes, his wives, and his concubines, drank in them.*
> [4] *They drank wine, and praised the gods of gold, and of silver, of brass, of iron, of wood, and of stone.*
> [5] *In the same hour came forth fingers of a man's hand, and wrote over against the candlestick upon the plaister of the wall of the king's palace: and the king saw the part of the hand that wrote.*
> [6] *Then the king's countenance was changed, and his thoughts troubled him, so that the joints of his loins were loosed, and his knees smote one against another.*
> [7] *The king cried aloud to bring in the astrologers, the Chaldeans, and the soothsayers. And the king spake, and said to the wise men of Babylon, Whosoever shall read this writing, and shew me the interpretation thereof, shall be clothed with scarlet, and have a chain of gold about his neck, and shall be the third ruler in the kingdom.*
> [8] *Then came in all the king's wise men: but they could not read the writing, nor make known to the king the interpretation thereof.*
> [9] *Then was king Belshazzar greatly troubled, and his countenance was changed in him, and his lords were astonied.*
> [10] *Now the queen by reason of the words of the king and his lords came into the banquet house: and the queen spake and said, O king, live for ever: let not thy thoughts trouble thee, nor let thy countenance be changed:*
> [11] *There is a man in thy kingdom, in whom is the spirit of the holy gods; and in the days of thy father* **light and understanding and wisdom, like the wisdom of the gods, was found in him;** *whom*

> the king Nebuchadnezzar thy father, the king, I say, thy father, made master of the magicians, astrologers, Chaldeans, and soothsayers;
> ¹² Forasmuch as an excellent spirit, and knowledge, and understanding, interpreting of dreams, and shewing of hard sentences, and dissolving of doubts, were found in the same Daniel, whom the king named Belteshazzar: now let Daniel be called, and he will shew the interpretation.
> ¹³ Then was Daniel brought in before the king. And the king spake and said unto Daniel, Art thou that Daniel, which art of the children of the captivity of Judah, whom the king my father brought out of Jewry?
> ¹⁴ I have even heard of thee, that the spirit of the gods is in thee, and **that light and understanding and excellent wisdom is found in thee.**
>
> Daniel 5: 1-14

The Knowledge of God lightens our spirit- man. Just as the Psalmist said – 'The entrance of your word gives light and understanding to the simple' (Psalm 119: 130). God's word is like an open door that lets in light or knowledge. Understanding is also light. On the day Jesus was raised back to life, He appeared to two disciples on their way to Emmaus and he expounded to them in all the scriptures the things concerning Him beginning at Moses and all the prophets. Interestingly, they did not understand a bit of all He had said not until there was an entrance of the Word into their hearts. They heard Him speak about the Law and the Prophets but could not make any sense out of it until their understanding was opened (light was released).

> ²⁷ And beginning at Moses and all the prophets, he expounded unto them in all the scriptures the things concerning himself.
> ⁴⁴ And he said unto them, These are the words which I spake unto you, while I was yet with you, that all things must be fulfilled, which were written in the law of Moses, and in the prophets, and in the psalms, concerning me.

> ⁴⁵ Then opened he their understanding, that they might understand the scriptures,
>
> Luke 24:27, 44-45

To the natural man, the true meaning of God's word is concealed. The seal must be broken in order to relate with the truth of God's word. The veil must be taken away to allow access to spiritual truth. We can therefore say that anyone void of the knowledge of God lives in darkness. In like manner, anyone that lacks understanding also lives in darkness.

> ⁴ In whom the god of this world hath blinded the minds of them which believe not, lest the light of the glorious gospel of Christ, who is the image of God, should shine unto them.
> ⁵ For we preach not ourselves, but Christ Jesus the Lord; and ourselves your servants for Jesus' sake.
> ⁶ For God, who commanded the light to shine out of darkness, hath shined in our hearts, to give the light of the knowledge of the glory of God in the face of Jesus Christ.
>
> 2 Corinthians 4:4-6

Chapter 4
WHEN LIGHT GOES DARK

We mentioned briefly, in an earlier chapter, the story of the woman who was caught in the act of adultery that the Bible describes in *John 8*. I think we need to revisit the story to gain an idea of what can happen when light goes dark. Looking through scriptures, if there is anything that transforms an atmosphere of light to one of darkness, it is sin. It was sin that caused Satan to be cast out of Heaven into darkness. It was sin that caused Adam and Eve to be thrown out of the garden of Eden. It was sin that separated the children of Israel from God and caused them to be taken into captivity.

If, truly, we have embraced the message that God is light, then we are joined to Him; we are partakers of His divine nature and do not have communion with darkness (*2 Corinthians 6:14*). If we walk in darkness, we cannot claim that we have received the message [*that was from the beginning – that God is light*]. A key question for someone could be, but what exactly does it mean to walk in darkness? To walk in darkness is to live in error, sin, or ignorance. Living in sin is different from falling into sin though. We cannot go on sinning so that grace may abound. Let me explain.

God is a gracious God and has made provision for us if we fall into sin, similar to that of the woman caught in the act of adultery but the Christian walk demands growth. As we grow in this light, it is almost inevitable, that at some point, we will miss the mark and require help. This act of falling is evidence that we need light. We are not meant to fall when there is light. People stumble in the absence of light. The Bible explains that Jesus is our advocate with the Father who will intercede on our behalf.

> [1] *My little children, these things I write to you,* **so that you may not sin.** *And if anyone sins, we have an Advocate with the Father, Jesus Christ the righteous.*
>
> 1 John 2:1

Look at that verse again. His intention is that we do not sin. However, "**if anyone sins, we have an Advocate.**" Wow! Is it not comforting to find out that God has made provision for when things do not necessarily go as we planned? Look at what the Apostle says, *"If we walk in the light as He is in the light, the blood of Jesus cleanses us from all our sins (1 John 1:7)."*

We can see from these scriptures that the picture painted here is not that of one who constantly stays in a fallen state. The picture is that of one who recognises sin for what it is and takes immediate action with the Advocate to cleanse sin.

Living in sin on the other hand represents someone who constantly intermingles with sin. Someone who does not recognise what they do as sin and therefore sees no need to make amendments. Unfortunately, many people hide under the umbrella of ignorance. Ignorance though, will not exempt from the consequences of sin. As is popularly said, ignorance of gravity does not mean you will not drop down to the ground if you jump off a cliff.

There was a time and season for which ignorance

was "*accepted*" but it now no longer tenable. While addressing the Areopagus, Paul explained to the men of Athens that our times of ignorance [the period prior to our experience of the saving knowledge of Christ] God overlooked.

> *30 Truly, these times of ignorance God overlooked, but now commands all men everywhere to repent,*
> *31 because He has appointed a day on which He will judge the world in righteousness by the Man whom He has ordained. He has given assurance of this to all by raising Him from the dead."*
>
> Acts 17:30-31 (NKJV)

Peter the Apostle too admonished us saying:

> *14 as obedient children, not conforming yourselves to the former lusts, as in your ignorance;*
>
> 1 Peter 1:14

Sin is darkness

> *1 Jesus went unto the mount of Olives.*
> *2 And early in the morning he came again into the temple, and all the people came unto him; and he sat down, and taught them.*
> *3 And the scribes and Pharisees brought unto him a woman taken in adultery; and when they had set her in the midst,*
> *4 They say unto him, Master, this woman was taken in adultery, in the very act.*
> *5 Now Moses in the law commanded us, that such should be stoned: but what sayest thou?*
> *6 This they said, tempting him, that they might have to accuse him. But Jesus stooped down, and with his finger wrote on the ground, as though he heard them not.*
> *7 So when they continued asking him, he lifted up himself, and said unto them, He that is without sin among you, let him first cast a stone at her.*
> *8 And again he stooped down, and wrote on the ground.*
> *9 And they which heard it, being convicted by their own conscience, went out one by one, beginning at the eldest, even unto the last:*

> *and Jesus was left alone, and the woman standing in the midst.*
> *¹⁰ When Jesus had lifted up himself, and saw none but the woman, he said unto her, Woman, where are those thine accusers? hath no man condemned thee?*
> *¹¹ She said, No man, Lord. And Jesus said unto her, Neither do I condemn thee: go, and sin no more.*
>
> John 8:1-11

Look at *verses 10 & 11* carefully and see what Jesus said. Was he condoning the sin? The obvious answer to that question is No. However, neither did He condemn her but gave the instruction *"...go, and sin no more.."* Jesus had shown what Light could do. Light makes mercy prevail over judgement. Since she had experienced the light of God, it appears that staying away from sin was a pre-requisite for the continual experience. Sin would have taken her back to groping in darkness. Sin is darkness. It is a loose-covering for evil deeds and shame.

For instance, when Adam and Eve sinned against God in the Garden of Eden, they sought for *"a place in the dark"* (they hid themselves), but even in the dark, light found them. Though they covered their shame with fig leaves they were still uncovered.

> *⁶ And when the woman saw that the tree was good for food, and that it was pleasant to the eyes, and a tree to be desired to make one wise, she took of the fruit thereof, and did eat, and gave also unto her husband with her; and he did eat.*
> *⁷ And the eyes of them both were opened, and they knew that they were naked; and they sewed fig leaves together, and made themselves aprons.*
> *⁸ **And they heard the voice of the Lord God walking in the garden in the cool of the day: and Adam and his wife hid themselves from the presence of the Lord God amongst the trees of the garden.***
>
> Genesis 3:6-8

Nothing is under cover when light comes. Everything is revealed! They thought they were covered, but everything was bare before God. Paul says:

> ¹³ But all things that are reproved are made manifest by the light: for whatsoever doth make manifest is light
>
> *Ephesians 5:13*

And the writer of Proverbs also says:

> ¹³ He that covereth his sins shall not prosper: but whoso confesseth and forsaketh them shall have mercy.
>
> *Proverbs 28:13*

We need not cover our sins because they will be exposed if not confessed. Grace is God's covering for sin. After Adam and Eve were unsuccessful in covering their nakedness as a result of sin, God now made a covering for them using tunics of skin (*Genesis 3:21*). Grace is God's effort to cover sin and not man's. The Psalmist says:

> ¹ Blessed is he whose transgression is forgiven, whose sin is covered.
> ² Blessed is the man unto **whom the Lord imputeth not iniquity, and in whose spirit there is no guile.**
>
> *Psalm 32: 1 - 2*

Covering of sin is not what God intends to do for us on a daily basis and that is why Christ came as the one-time sacrifice. By the reason of His death and resurrection, we have been clothed - covered - by grace. Paul said *'What shall we say then? Shall we continue in sin that grace may abound? Certainly not! How shall we who died to sin live any longer in it?'* – Romans 6:1-2.

It is hard to kick against the pricks

Darkness cannot judge Darkness. A house divided against itself shall not stand. Only Light can judge darkness. Light shines in darkness and darkness cannot comprehend it. Darkness disappears when light comes up. No matter the intensity of light you have around you, it will always prevail over darkness.

Saul of Tarsus was a man who lived in darkness and his deeds were evil. He legalised his fight against The Light but did not prevail. He finally lost the battle to Light on his way to Damascus to persecute the followers of the Light. This is the Light John testified about in his book saying, *'This Light shines in darkness and darkness could not comprehend [overcome, apprehend, extinguish, overtake, overpower] it – John 1:5 (AMP)*. Paul's experience with this Light was also described in scriptures

> [6] *And it came to pass, that, as I made my journey, and was come nigh unto Damascus about noon, suddenly there shone from heaven a great light round about me.*
> [7] *And I fell unto the ground, and heard a voice saying unto me, Saul, Saul, why persecutest thou me?*
> [8] *And I answered, Who art thou, Lord? And he said unto me, I am Jesus of Nazareth, whom thou persecutest.*
> [9] *And they that were with me saw indeed the light, and were afraid; but they heard not the voice of him that spake to me.*
> [10] *And I said, What shall I do, LORD? And the Lord said unto me, Arise, and go into Damascus; and there it shall be told thee of all things which are appointed for thee to do.*
> [11] *And when I could not see for the glory of that light, being led by the hand of them that were with me, I came into Damascus.*
>
> Acts 22:6-11
>
> [12] *Whereupon as I went to Damascus with authority and commission from the chief priests,*
> [13] *At midday, O king, I saw in the way a light from heaven, above the brightness of the sun, shining round about me and them which journeyed with me.*
> [14] *And when we were all fallen to the earth, I heard a voice speaking unto me, and saying in the Hebrew tongue, Saul, Saul, why*

> *persecutest thou me? it is hard for thee to kick against the pricks.*
> ¹⁵ *And I said, Who art thou, Lord? And he said, I am Jesus whom thou persecutest.*
>
> Acts 26:12-15

Light overpowered Paul and he became an instrument of light. He discovered that darkness could not prevail over light and in his letter to the Corinthians he said, *'but we can do nothing against the truth but for the truth'* (*2 Corinthians 13:8*). Fighting the truth of the Gospel is a battle that can never be won by the devil. Kicking against the pricks is a pretty hard thing to do. The Greek word for pricks, *kentron,* is also translated as goads. A goad is a long-pointed stick used for prodding cattle or other animals. A goad has a pointed piece of iron clasped to its end and an animal that kicks against the goads will only wound itself. It is therefore a silly, unwise and reckless thing to kick against the goads. Simply put, this means that it is foolish to kick against a powerful authority.

Growing up as a young boy, I was very stubborn and I always ended up being severely punished. It was foolishness on my part to kick against elders because I got punished each time. The cycle of kicking against authorities and getting battered was terminated by Christ when he took over the lordship of my heart and life.

All authority has been given to Christ in heaven and on earth (*Matthew 28:18*). Jesus is the most powerful authority both on earth and in heaven and rebelling against Him is indeed a difficult thing.

While Saul, also called Paul, and Barnabas were preaching at Cyprus, the proconsul requested that they should come and share God's word with him, but with him was Elymas the sorcerer who perverted the ways of the LORD - *kicking against the goads.*

> ⁶ And when they had gone through the isle unto Paphos, they found a certain sorcerer, a false prophet, a Jew, whose name was Barjesus:
> ⁷ Which was with the deputy of the country, Sergius Paulus, a prudent man; who called for Barnabas and Saul, and desired to hear the word of God.
> ⁸ But Elymas the sorcerer (for so is his name by interpretation) withstood them, seeking to turn away the deputy from the faith.
> ⁹ Then Saul, (who also is called Paul,) filled with the Holy Ghost, set his eyes on him.
> ¹⁰ And said, O full of all subtilty and all mischief, thou child of the devil, thou enemy of all righteousness, wilt thou not cease to pervert the right ways of the Lord?
> ¹¹ And now, behold, the hand of the Lord is upon thee, and thou shalt be blind, not seeing the sun for a season. And immediately there fell on him a mist and a darkness; and he went about seeking some to lead him by the hand.
> ¹² Then the deputy, when he saw what was done, believed, being astonished at the doctrine of the Lord.
>
> Acts 13:6-12

Elymas kicked against the goads and he was dealt with accordingly. Another good example is Pharaoh. All that was required of him was to let Israel leave Egypt. Just a decree to that effect would suffice. Now I remember vividly as a child, occasions when I would be asked to do a particular thing and I would refuse to do it. However, my father would send someone else to me with the message *"tell him that is my instruction."* I dared not disobey after hearing that. Eight times the LORD God sent Moses to Pharaoh saying, *"Let my people go that they may serve me"* and he blatantly refused. He disdained God. He replied Moses saying *"Who is the LORD that I should obey His voice to let Israel go?"* (Exodus 5:2). That was gross disobedience! Students are often expelled for gross disobedience. Pharaoh was not only expelled from his throne, he was destroyed (*Psalm 136:15*).

Lucifer also kicked against the goads was expelled from heaven and was condemned eternally (*Isaiah 14: 12-15; Revelation 12:7-12*). Also remember that when Adam and Eve kicked against God's authority, He drove them out of Eden (*Genesis 3:22-24*).

You will agree that Paul's persecution of followers of the Way,Pharaoh rebellion, Lucifer's rebellion and Adam and Eve's disobedience were all dangerous things to do. The same applies to us if we kick against the authority of Christ in our lives. If you kick against His authority, you get kicked out of His sight. But if we obey His commandments, we will abide in His love (*John 15:10*).

> [21] *He that hath my commandments, and keepeth them, he it is that loveth me: and he that loveth me shall be loved of my Father, and I will love him, and will manifest myself to him.*
>
> John 14:21

All that is required of us as children of Light is to trust and obey.

The truth of the Gospel is light

Men can be deceived by lies but the truth cannot be changed and will definitely be made manifest. When the truth eventually manifests, it overpowers every lie that had gone ahead. Truth remains a formidable force that cannot be conquered. An old African proverb states that '*No matter how long lies travel, it will certainly be overtaken by truth*'.

Today, Christians all over the world celebrate the death and resurrection of the Christ. It is awesome to experience the saving knowledge of our Lord Jesus Christ. The life, death and resurrection of the Christ speak of Him as the Son of God yet the world refused to acknowledge this truth. In fact, He was tested and tempted in order to validate the truth of His Sonship. Let's briefly consider the life, death and resurrection of Christ and the power of truth.

Before His days in the flesh, several prophecies were said about Him. One of the revelations about His identity that was told Mary was that the child she will give birth to is the Son of God

> [35] And the angel answered and said unto her, The Holy Ghost shall come upon thee, and the power of the Highest shall overshadow thee: therefore also that holy thing which shall be born of thee shall be called the Son of God.
>
> Luke 1:35

When it was about time to start His ministry, He was tempted by the devil to show Himself as the Son of God. In all temptations, the devil said, *'if you are the Son of God...'* (Matthew 4:1-11; Luke 4:1-13). Jesus rebuked the devil as He well understood his evil mission. During His ministry, demons and evil spirits identified Him (*Mark 3:11; 5:7*).

> [11] And unclean spirits, when they saw him, fell down before him, and cried, saying, Thou art the Son of God.
>
> Mark 3:11

> [7] And cried with a loud voice, and said, What have I to do with thee, Jesus, thou Son of the most high God? I adjure thee by God, that thou torment me not.
>
> Mark 5:7

His disciples were filled with awe after He calmed the

storm and said, *Truly, He is the Son of God (Matthew 14:33)*. Even though His disciples once confessed that He was the Son of God, it was Peter that caught the revelation of His identity.

> *¹³ When Jesus came into the coasts of Caesarea Philippi, he asked his disciples, saying, Whom do men say that I the Son of man am?*
> *¹⁴ And they said, Some say that thou art John the Baptist: some, Elias; and others, Jeremias, or one of the prophets.*
> *¹⁵ He saith unto them, But whom say ye that I am?*
> *¹⁶ And Simon Peter answered and said, Thou art the Christ, the Son of the living God.*
>
> Matthew 16:13-16

The only strong evidence the Jews had against Jesus in order to crucify Him was the fact that He said to them that He is the Son of God. Of course they knew the truth, but they would not acknowledge it. It was too hard for them to believe. They had previously tried to kill Him at two different occasions because of this same reason but their plot to kill him did not succeed *(John 5:16 – 18; 10: 31 – 38)*. And finally, they found a good place to use their evidence against Him after Pilate declared openly that he found no fault in Him.

> *⁷ The Jews answered him, We have a law, and by our law he ought to die, because he made himself the Son of God.*
>
> John 19:7

While He was on the cross He was mocked that if He is the Son of God, He should save Himself *(Matthew 27:40, 43)*. When He finally gave up the ghost, the Centurion that witnessed His suffering and death concluded by saying *'Truly, He is the Son of God'* - *Matthew 27: 54*.

The truth of the Gospel is that Jesus died and was raised back to life on the third day by the power of God, but the devil used the Chief priests and the elders to bribe the soldiers that guarded his tomb saying that Jesus' body was stolen by His disciples. This lie is still commonly reported among the Jews until this day (*Matthew 28:11-15*).

The devil is working hard to make sure men do not believe in the truth. As children of light, let us preach the truth of the Gospel to every creature so that the glorious light of the Gospel will shine over their hearts. The end will come after we have declared the truth of the Gospel to all nations (*Mark 13:10*). God wants us to help others discover the true meaning of life. The truth of the Gospel unveils the mystery of life. Jesus came that we may have life in abundance.

Chapter 5
YOU ARE THE LIGHT OF THE WORLD

> *14 Ye are the light of the world. A city that is set on an hill cannot be hid.*
> *15 Neither do men light a candle, and put it under a bushel, but on a candlestick; and it giveth light unto all that are in the house.*
> *16 Let your light so shine before men, that they may see your good works, and glorify your Father which is in heaven.*
>
> Matthew 5:14-16

So far, we have talked about God being light, we have seen some of the attributes of light and of course, we have an idea of what the world could look like in the absence of light. One thing all these thoughts have in common is that they consider God and the things God made but what about man? If God is light and God made man by using Himself as a template, should man not have some of the very same characteristics of God? The very thought of this is mind-blowing.

I am sure that, by now, you have realised that the Bible is the basis of the thoughts that are being shared with you in this book and the reason is because Paul was clear to Timothy when he said *'All scripture is given by the inspiration of God'* (2 Timothy 3:16). This places God in the position of the Author of scriptures and gives weight to the words captured in it.

When Jesus came the world, He did not only come to pronounce Himself as the Light of the World. He also came to pronounce those that accept Him as the starting authority in their lives, the light of the world. This is clearly stated in *verse 14* above. Wow! I think this actually deserves a pause for reflection. Thinking of ourselves in this light also changes our perspective on light.

Sons of Light

We have earlier described a life without Christ to be dark, void and empty. This was the former state of things before the glorious light of the Gospel shone upon our hearts. When we received the Word of life, God re-positioned us in the Spirit to be lights in our world. We became sons of light the moment we believed in Jesus.

> [36] *While you have the light, believe in the light, that you may become sons of light." These things Jesus spoke, and departed, and was hidden from them.*
>
> John 12:36 (NKJV)
>
> [8] *For you were once darkness, but now you are light in the Lord. Walk as children of light*
>
> Ephesians 5:8 (NKJV)

Did you notice that Paul did not say that we were in darkness; instead he said, '*you were **once** darkness*'. When we heard the Word of Truth and embraced Christ, we became light. Hallelujah! 'We are the light of the world, a city set on a hill which cannot be hidden'.

We are to reflect Him

In the study of the earth commonly known as Geography, we were told that during the day while the sun gives its light on the earth, the moon and the stars are not seen but are positioned such that they receive light from the sun. The light of the moon that we see at night is a reflection of the light of the sun. The moon is the brightest object in the sky after the sun. I use this analogy because a prophecy of the prophet Malachi describes Jesus as the Sun of righteousness .(*Malachi 4:2*) We as children of God can accurately position ourselves in God so as to draw light from Him.

We are to reflect His light in the world. Even if the sun is not physically available at night, the moon can still give light to the world. That is, even if Christ is not physically present here on earth, you and I should be His ambassadors. We should express Him to the world. This is a present-day assignment of the Church. Just as Jesus described Himself as the Light of the world, we are also the light of the world.

> [17] *Herein is our love made perfect, that we may have boldness in the day of judgment:* ***because as he is, so are we in this world.***
>
> 1 John 4:17

Apart from Christ, Christians are the only people that can shine so brightly in this dark world. Light is meant to be conspicuous especially in a dark environment where it cannot be hidden. We are indeed the light of the world. We need to arise and shine in the world because darkness has covered the earth and deep darkness the people.

Light shines in darkness

It is a natural characteristic of light to shine in darkness. In fact, one of the only ways you know natural light exists somewhere is the fact that it allows you to see with your eyes. For example, if a blind person is in a room and you put a painting on the wall, it does not matter whether the lights are on or off, that blind person will not see what is in the room.

I believe a key reason the light of some Christians have not shone like they should is because their light is not too different from the other light in the world. So, even though they are there, nobody knows the difference.

The book of Revelation talks about the Church in a place called Pergamos, a city very much given to idolatry that the Bible describes the place as a place *"where Satan dwells."* It was an aphorism among the Jews, that in a place where the law of God was not learnt or studied, there Satan dwelt; but he was obliged to leave the place where a synagogue or academy was established. So you can imagine the kind of persecution the Church must have faced. In spite of these, Jesus still had a charge against them – they were involved in idolatry and immorality and Jesus addressed that in His message to the Church.

> *[12] "And to the angel of the church in Pergamos write, 'These things says He who has the sharp two-edged sword:*
> *[13] "I know your works, and where you dwell, where Satan's throne is. And you hold fast to My name, and did not deny My faith even in the days in which Antipas was My faithful martyr, who was killed among you, where Satan dwells.*
> *[14] But I have a few things against you, because you have there those who hold the doctrine of Balaam, who taught Balak to put a stumbling block before the children of Israel, to eat things sacrificed to idols, and to commit sexual immorality.*
> *[15] Thus you also have those who hold the doctrine of the Nicolaitans, which thing I hate.*
> *[16] Repent, or else I will come to you quickly and will fight against them with the sword of My mouth.*
> *[17] "He who has an ear, let him hear what the Spirit says to the churches. To him who overcomes I will give some of the hidden manna to eat. And I will give him a white stone, and on the stone a new name written which no one knows except him who receives it."'*
>
> Revelation 2: 12-17

The spirit of excellence in Daniel was a light that shone in Babylon. He was outstanding in the entire region. His light drew kings and men to God. The Church is a very influential component of society. When darkness prevails in a society, the Church is said to be losing - or has lost - its influence and therefore her power of illumination. The environment may be very challenging but light will always shine in darkness.

Similarly, the Church today is in the midst of a perverse world. Christians are being persecuted, men have enthroned abominations in their hearts in place of Christ, some ungodly men, systems, and values have crept into our local assemblies turning the grace of our God into licentiousness denying the only Lord God and our Lord Jesus Christ (*Jude 1:4*). We are in the world but we should not be influenced by the systems and values of the world. We should not conform to the world. God knows and understands the pressures of the times we live in but He needs us to understand that by the power that is available in us we are able to subdue the systems of the world. We cannot afford to compromise our position in the society. We are the light of the world.

Walking in the light

We have been repositioned by Christ so that we can receive light from Him. We need to maintain this position by walking in the light. The word *'walk'* is often used to mean conduct or life. Walking in the light therefore means not living in the error of sin.

> [7] *But if we walk in the light as He is in the light, we have fellowship with one another, and the blood of Jesus Christ His Son cleanses us from all sin.*
>
> 1 John 1:7

A popular hymn I learnt as a child explains the Christian life as walking in the light – *"When we walk with the Lord in the light of His word...*" To walk in the light is to lead a life of holiness by not living in the error of sin. It suggests that walking in the light also means walking in the truth – clinging unto the truth and living the truth even in the midst of opposition. The devil has so dominated the hearts of men such that truth is hardly represented in our day-to-day lives. Just like Isaiah prophesied, *"Truth has fallen dead in the streets, truth fails and he who departs from evil makes himself a prey" (Isaiah 59:14-15)*. As children of light, we must walk in the truth. The Church is the ground and pillar of the truth and should live as such.

Following the Light

To shine as light in our world, truth must be supported and maintained by the church both in doctrine and conduct. Living requires following the Light of the world. Man on his own and by himself cannot live without following God who is Light and the Author of life. Man *(represented in Adam and Eve)* fell in the beginning when he chose not to follow the instruction of God. So when God (Light) appeared in the garden, Adam and Eve hid themselves. They preferred to hide "in the dark" by covering their nakedness from the beams of light shed upon the garden by the presence of God. Of course God's light located them and instead of leaves God covered them with sheepskin.

Jesus is the light of the world and in John 8:12, He assures whoever follows Him will not to walk in darkness. As explained earlier, following God is very important. He is the Shepherd of our souls. He will always lead us in the path of righteousness. Yes, even if it appears that death has cast its shadows on the path. It seems dark, gloomy and lonely; our confidence is that God is with us. We can absolutely trust God with the journey of our lives.

¹ *The Lord is my shepherd; I shall not want.*
² *He maketh me to lie down in green pastures: he leadeth me beside the still waters.*
³ *He restoreth my soul: he leadeth me in the paths of righteousness for his name's sake.*
⁴ *Yea, though I walk through the valley of the shadow of death, I will fear no evil: for thou art with me; thy rod and thy staff they comfort me*

Psalm 23:1-4

¹ *But now thus saith the Lord that created thee, O Jacob, and he that formed thee, O Israel, Fear not: for I have redeemed thee, I have called thee by thy name; thou art mine.*
² *When thou passest through the waters, I will be with thee; and through the rivers, they shall not overflow thee: when thou walkest through the fire, thou shalt not be burned; neither shall the flame kindle upon thee.*

Isaiah 43:1-2

Life may present us with some of its gloomy scenes, but we can be assured of God's guidance throughout the period until we eventually see light at the end of the tunnel. *"He will never leave nor forsake us"*

Chapter 6
BENEFITS OF LIGHT

Light has a very interesting nature and I think the best was to describe this is to use an analogy. Imagine you are in a dark art gallery filled with precious paintings at night and the lights are turned off. You look in front of you, sideways and turn around and you see nothing. Does this remove the fact that you have precious paintings in the room? In that moment, the only thing that stands between you and the appreciation of the precious painting is one thing. Light.

Many people live life like I have just described above. The tragedy, though, is that while they have all their physical senses active, they do not see the precious things "paintings" of life around themselves. They do not see the great opportunity God has presented before them because the god of this world, the devil, has blinded their eyes but when the light of the Gospel of Christ shines through to them, what will they see?

There are a few things I believe people will see. Let us look at a few of these.

Wisdom
Wisdom is a product of light. Wisdom is an expression of light. Wisdom is guaranteed once the light of God shines upon our heart. This was evident in the life of Job whom at a young age had his seat at the open square. His fellow young men hid when they saw him; the aged arose and stood; princes refrained from talking and they

put their hands on their mouth; the voice of nobles was hushed and their tongue stuck to the roof of their mouth. Job attributed all these to the wisdom at work in his life by the reason of God's light that shone upon him.

> *² Oh that I were as in months past, as in the days when God preserved me;*
> *³ When his candle shined upon my head, and when by his light I walked through darkness;*
>
> Job 29:2-3

Wisdom is needed for us to walk in God's programme for our lives. We need to walk in wisdom all the days of our lives in order for us to fulfil our part in God's eternal purpose. The Psalmist while considering the frailty of man said *"The days of our lives are seventy years, and if by reason of strength they are eighty years, yet their boast is only labour and sorrow; for it is soon cut off and we fly away. Who knows the power of Your anger? For as the fear of You, so is Your wrath. So teach us to number our days that we may gain a heart of wisdom"* (Psalm 90:10-12).

Our weakness and imperfection as men can be transformed to strength through wisdom. **A heart of wisdom is what we need to live a life of purpose**. Paul the Apostle admonished us to walk circumspectly not as fools but as wise; redeeming the time because the days are evil. Wisdom helps us understand what the will of the Lord is.

> *¹⁵ See then that ye walk circumspectly, not as fools, but as wise,*
> *¹⁶ Redeeming the time, because the days are evil.*
> *¹⁷ Wherefore be ye not unwise, but understanding what the will of the Lord is.*
>
> Ephesians 5: 15-17

We live in a time just like in the days of Daniel when

only wisdom can guarantee life. Nebuchadnezzar had given a command to destroy all the wise men of Babylon because they became "ordinary" men when he needed them the most. In those days, wise men in Babylon were magicians, astrologers and soothsayers. Daniel, Hananiah, Mishael and Azariah were grouped with these men. No one could change the king's exigent decree; their death sentence has been signed:

> [14] Then with counsel and wisdom Daniel answered Arioch, the captain of the king's guard, who had gone out to kill the wise men of Babylon;
> [15] he answered and said to Arioch the king's captain, "Why is the decree from the king so urgent?" Then Arioch made the decision known to Daniel.
> [16] So Daniel went in and asked the king to give him time, that he might tell the king the interpretation.
> [17] Then Daniel went to his house, and made the decision known to Hananiah, Mishael, and Azariah, his companions,
> [18] that they might seek mercies from the God of heaven concerning this secret, so that Daniel and his companions might not perish with the rest of the wise men of Babylon. [19] Then the secret was revealed to Daniel in a night vision. So Daniel blessed the God of heaven.
> [20] Daniel answered and said: "Blessed be the name of God forever and ever, For wisdom and might are His.
> [21] And He changes the times and the seasons; He removes kings and raises up kings; He gives wisdom to the wise And knowledge to those who have understanding.
> [22] He reveals deep and secret things; He knows what is in the darkness, And light dwells with Him.
> [23] "I thank You and praise You, O God of my fathers; You have given me wisdom and might, And have now made known to me what we asked of You, For You have made known to us the king's demand."
>
> *Daniel 2: 14-23*

The wisdom of God distinguished Daniel, Hananiah,

Mishael and Azariah from the so-called wise men of Babylon. So also, the wisdom of God will distinguish you from the seemingly wise men of this world. The wisdom of God will reveal to you solutions that the world cannot give. Beyond the ordinary, God will give you a mouth and a wisdom that none of your adversary can gainsay in Jesus' name. Amen.

Solomon was blessed with wisdom and it was recorded that he spoke three thousand proverbs; his songs were a thousand and five; he spoke of different kind of trees; he spoke of animals, birds, fish and of creeping things. Men from all over the world came to hear his wisdom.

> [33] *And he spake of trees, from the cedar tree that is in Lebanon even unto the hyssop that springeth out of the wall: he spake also of beasts, and of fowl, and of creeping things, and of fishes.*
> [34] *And there came of all people to hear the wisdom of Solomon, from all kings of the earth, which had heard of his wisdom.*
>
> 1 Kings 4: 33-34

Yes, he was so blessed with wisdom that he composed witty aphorisms with things he saw. But Solomon in all his wisdom still had things too wonderful for him – the way of a ship in the ocean, the way of an eagle in the sky, the way of a serpent on the rock and the way of a man with a maid! (*Proverbs 30:18-19*).

When Jesus came to the earth, He said... "*A greater than Solomon is here*". (*Luke 11:31*). In other words, a dimension deeper than Solomon's wisdom is here. Paul went further to explain in his letter to the church in Corinth that Christ is the wisdom of God (*1 Corinthians 1:24*). He is the wisdom that answers all things. Wisdom is not just the application of accumulated knowledge gained through experience; **Christ is Wisdom**. All the treasures of wisdom and knowledge are hidden in him (*Colossians 2:3*). He was there with God in the beginning. He was instrumental in the creation; for nothing was made without Him (*Proverbs 8:22-31*).

Oh we need Christ, the Wisdom and the Power of God. He is the key to living life to the fullest. He is the key to living a 'superior' life. Daniel was ten times better than his mates. Not even the so-called astrologers or wise men in Babylon could match him because God gave him a mouth and wisdom no man could gainsay. Go get wisdom, seek after her and she will exalt you. He that lacks wisdom let him ask God who gives liberally for the Lord gives wisdom and out of his mouth comes understanding.

Light – A tool for discerning the timing of God's programme

> [15] And on the day that the tabernacle was reared up the cloud covered the tabernacle, namely, the tent of the testimony: and at even there was upon the tabernacle as it were the appearance of fire, until the morning.
> [16] So it was alway: the cloud covered it by day, and the appearance of fire by night.
> [17] And when the cloud was taken up from the tabernacle, then after that the children of Israel journeyed: and in the place where the cloud abode, there the children of Israel pitched their tents.
> [18] At the commandment of the LORD the children of Israel journeyed, and at the commandment of the LORD they pitched: as long as the cloud abode upon the tabernacle they rested in their tents.
> [19] And when the cloud tarried long upon the tabernacle many days, then the children of Israel kept the charge of the LORD, and journeyed not.
> [20] And so it was, when the cloud was a few days upon the tabernacle; according to the commandment of the LORD they abode in their tents, and according to the commandment of the LORD they journeyed.
> [21] And so it was, when the cloud abode from even unto the morning,

> *and that the cloud was taken up in the morning, then they journeyed: whether it was by day or by night that the cloud was taken up, they journeyed.*
> *²² Or whether it were two days, or a month, or a year, that the cloud tarried upon the tabernacle, remaining thereon, the children of Israel abode in their tents, and journeyed not: but when it was taken up, they journeyed.*
> *²³ At the commandment of the LORD they rested in the tents, and at the commandment of the LORD they journeyed: they kept the charge of the LORD, at the commandment of the LORD by the hand of Moses.*
>
> Numbers 9:15-23

When God led the children of Israel out of Egypt, He did so with the Pillar of Cloud by day and the Pillar of fire by night. He went further by dictating their movement using the cloud. When the cloud comes down then the children knows that it is time for them to camp, and when the cloud lifts, and then it is time to continue the journey. They could discern God's timing via the operation of light (cloud).

It is very important that we discern times and seasons. Discerning times and seasons require an understanding of the operations of light.

> *¹⁴ And God said, Let there be lights in the firmament of the heaven to divide the day from the night; and let them be for signs, and for seasons, and for days, and years:*
> *¹⁵ And let them be for lights in the firmament of the heaven to give light upon the earth: and it was so.*
> *¹⁶ And God made two great lights; the greater light to rule the day, and the lesser light to rule the night: he made the stars also.*
>
> Genesis 1:14-16

Life has been structured by God into different seasons. For instance, the four temperate seasons in the earth - spring, summer, autumn and winter are regulated by light. Summer is the warmest of the four seasons. During this season, the days are the longest while the nights are the shortest. The length of the day decreases as the season evolves after the solstice. It goes on like that till winter, the coldest season of the year with the longest nights and shortest days. Likewise, our lives are regulated by God [Remember God is light]. We cannot live life to the fullest without Him. We cannot fulfil purpose without Him. Man will continue to grope in darkness and will live in confusion until he is connected to the Light that regulates our lives. Jesus is the Light through which we can discern God's timing for our lives. He will guide us so as not to go a step ahead of His time nor later than His time. His timing is accurate just as the common saying that 'God's time is the best'.

What to do with what you discover

We must learn from the beginning, that is, we must learn and understand God's original plan and how to align our lives with His plan. We must learn from The Beginning (Christ) and also retain the truth we have learnt from Him. John the beloved said "If what you heard from the beginning abides in you, you will abide in the Son and in the Father (1 John 2:24). Let His word dwell richly in you (Colossians 3:16); hide His word in your heart (Psalm 119:11); give more earnest heed to His words lest they slip (Hebrews 2:1); buy the truth and do not sell it (Proverbs 23:23).

> [1]"That which was from the beginning, which we have heard, which we have seen with our eyes, which we have looked upon, and our hands have handled, concerning the Word of life—"
>
> John 1:1

As mentioned earlier, the beginning is Christ. He can be heard, seen and touched. This means He is real! We can relate with the reality of God. Yes, we can hear Him, see Him and handle Him. God is not a mystic force somewhere in the sky. When His light shines upon our hearts, we will have access to Him. Light enables us to see Him. Light makes possible the knowledge of Him. The degree of light in you determines how much you know God. Light will further establish our relationship with Jesus.

Chapter 7
BE PREPARED

35 "Let your waist be girded and your lamps burning;
36 and you yourselves be like men who wait for their master, when he will return from the wedding, that when he comes and knocks they may open to him immediately.
37 Blessed are those servants whom the master, when he comes, will find watching. Assuredly, I say to you that he will gird himself and have them sit down to eat, and will come and serve them.
38 And if he should come in the second watch, or come in the third watch, and find them so, blessed are those servants. 39 But know this, that if the master of the house had known what hour the thief would come, he would have watched and not allowed his house to be broken into.
40 Therefore you also be ready, for the Son of Man is coming at an hour you do not expect."

Luke 12:35-40

The Boys' Scout motto, 'Be prepared' is explained to mean being ready both in mind and in body to duty. Scouts are taught to be disciplined, strong and active; being able to do the right thing at the right time.

Similarly as Christians, we have been taught to endure hardship as good soldiers of Christ (*2 Timothy 2:3*). We are to live in readiness for the coming of our Lord. When going on a journey, a traveller must be prepared. A person going to Antarctica does not go dressed like it is summer. We also need to make sure we get ourselves ready for the journey to our Maker. This is a journey not based on the attire worn but on the state of the heart. We need to lay aside every weight, and the sin which so easily ensnares us so that we can run with endurance and good speed the race that is set before us (*Hebrews 12:1*).

We need to constantly live our lives as a servant expecting his master who has been on a long journey to arrive at any moment. Our lamps need to be burning so our eyes can see the master as he approaches. I have heard it said before that preparation is the evidence of expectation.

One thing we need to remember about preparation is that preparation is not really something you do just before the Master comes. Preparation starts way before the Master comes. God is also not unreasonable, he gives us indications of His coming through the prophets he has sent.

The night is nearly over

> [12] *The night is nearly over; the day is almost here. So let us put aside the deeds of darkness and put on the armor of light.*
>
> Romans 13:12 (NIV)

Notice the writer says, "*The night is nearly over;*" the day of the Lord is almost here. As we know, night is the period of darkness between sunrise and sunset. In the above verse, night is the period preceding the fulfilment of the prophecy concerning the second coming of Christ. The appearance of Christ is the ultimate salvation spoken of by Peter:

> [9] *receiving the end of your faith—the salvation of your souls.*
> [10] *Of this salvation the prophets have inquired and searched carefully, who prophesied of the grace that would come to you,*
> [11] *searching what, or what manner of time, the Spirit of Christ who was in them was indicating when He testified beforehand the sufferings of Christ and the glories that would follow.*
> [12] *To them it was revealed that, not to themselves, but to us they were*

ministering the things which now have been reported to you through those who have preached the gospel to you by the Holy Spirit sent from heaven—things which angels desire to look into.

1 Peter 1:9-12 (NKJV)

This salvation is likened to a new day. It is referred to as the "Day of the Lord." The day Christ will be revealed to us in His full glory at His second coming. A day that is approaching faster than most people think. The expectation of the day of the Lord should instil in us the desire and willingness to put away works of darkness and to put on the armour of light – living a pure and holy life. We are to live in this continued state of expectancy of the Lord's coming. Paul, in his first epistle to the Thessalonians, explained that we are also children of the day; we are not of the night or of darkness.

> *[5] You are all sons of light and sons of the day. We are not of the night nor of darkness.*
> *[6] Therefore let us not sleep, as others do, but let us watch and be sober.*
> *[7] For those who sleep, sleep at night, and those who get drunk are drunk at night.*
> *[8] But let us who are of the day be sober, putting on the breastplate of faith and love, and as a helmet the hope of salvation.*
>
> *1 Thessalonians 5:5-8 (NKJV)*

Our salvation gives us the hope that Christ will surely return for the bride He purchased with His blood. The day of the Lord comes as a *'thief in the night'*. This means that the day comes suddenly and unexpectedly. But as uncertain as the day is, it will not come as a surprise to the children of light. We will be on our watch, waiting, hoping and preparing for His coming.

Jesus told us the parable of the ten virgins. They were all virgins (*holy and undefiled*), they all had lamps (light), they all were expecting the bridegroom, they all got so tired of waiting that they slept off, they all woke up when it was announced that the bridegroom was around, but not all of them had oil to sustain their light. Though they were virgins, they slept off. This denotes spiritual torpor. But even while they were asleep the bridegroom did not come suddenly to them. The Bible records that there was a cry at midnight, and it was the cry that woke the virgins.

> [6] "And at midnight a cry was heard: 'Behold, the bridegroom is coming; go out to meet him!'
> [7] Then all those virgins arose and trimmed their lamps.
>
> Matthew 25:6-7 (NKJV)

Even at midnight we are meant to be awake and watchful. Our lamps must be trimmed to meet the Bridegroom. The evidence of your expectation is in the trimming of your lamp. The revelation of the birth of Jesus was also given to shepherds who weren't sleeping at night but were watching over their sheep. They had the privilege of getting first-hand news of the birth of Jesus. So also will the second coming of Jesus be revealed to men watching and waiting at *'night'*.

The cry went out to the virgins because they were asleep. Just like it was in the days of Noah, God has placed criers in the world today to announce the coming of His Son and to warn men of eternal destruction. The rich man that was cast into hell in one Jesus' parable requested that Lazarus should be sent to his family to confirm the truth of this eternal destruction, but Abraham said to him that they have Moses and the prophets there for them to listen to.

> [27] "Then he said, 'I beg you therefore, father, that you would send him to my father's house,
> [28] for I have five brothers, that he may testify to them, lest they also come to this place of torment.'

²⁹ *Abraham said to him, 'They have Moses and the prophets; let them hear them.'*

Luke 16:27-29

God has strategically placed His servants in the world to announce to mankind that He is coming again. This is to give us time to wake up from our sleep, trim our lamps and come out to meet Him. You can't go in to meet with the bridegroom without your lamps trimmed on. Light is our guide to eternal life and the night is nearly over.